Wild Life

Wild Life

James McDermott

Nine
Arches
Press

Wild Life
James McDermott

ISBN: 978-1-913437-70-1
eISBN: 978-1-913437-71-8

First published June 2023 by:

Nine Arches Press
Unit 14, Sir Frank Whittle Business Centre,
Great Central Way, Rugby.
CV21 3XH
United Kingdom

www.ninearchespress.com

Printed on recycled paper in the United Kingdom by:
Imprint Digital

Nine Arches Press is supported using public funding by Arts Council England.

Contents

Closet

an average person's skin covers two square
metres   the standard height of a closet

age six   I open Mum's wardrobe door to
a den of furs   coven of black dresses

yellow brick road of snakeskin shoes   I gaze
into caves of high heels   eyes   see me   wink

I find myself sliding into a bruise
-plum dress   I turn my lips wound-red   my eyes

black   blue   in the mirror   I see father
appear   kick off my heels   rub out my face

tear at my frock   skin my new-born body
alive   trying to find muscle beneath

Joe

I remember being thirteen and Joe
when your closet opened at school   I was

the first to grab you like cigarettes
smoke with you behind bins   to mark your flesh

with fag   the first to touch hairs on your head
as dark as shame   as chocolate   I was

the one who kept calling you queer as I
wanted to scream that word out loud   that word

I was too clench-fisted to brand myself
in case I became as disgraceful as having

to wear shorts from lost property   I gobbed
on you to hide from lads who spat me out

when I emerged   you'd left by then   I can't
shake the taste of your hair out of my mind

Intestines

September 3rd 2005   ten past twelve   period four
I spew my guts on the school sports-hall floor
my intestines are athletic
they move food with a wave-like pattern
of muscular actions   peristalsis
I know what I want derives from the Greek
my thoughts   long hollowed coiled tubes
that lead to the anus   fit boys
call me faggot   a type of food
the intestines absorb the nutrients
then force out waste into the rectum
where nerves create sensations that make you
feel like a shit   but I cannot pass
it gathers in the stomach   my second brain
it makes me bottom heavy   shuttlecock
it piles until it fills my liver   heart
lungs   oesophagus   oral cavity
it makes me sick
humans breathe about twenty-five thousand times a day
humans are the only animal to blush

Seed

I am thirteen when at the urinals a boy
brushes my hand with his

then gestures with his head
to the cubicles

I want
to go in there with him

but tremor at being
caught in the act

I sweat that he might give
me HIV

I sweat that he might take
my phone   wallet   my life

holding it in
my hand like a knife

I shake wishing
I wouldn't waste my youth thinking

every boy who wants me   wants to hurt me
when he might just want me

or maybe   I am not scared of the boy
but scared of having a body that wants

to do things with other boys'
bodies

he zips his fly up quick   flees
leaves me gripping my manhood   small as

a seedling   waiting to be
planted   watered   to grow   to fruit

The Weight

after torrin a. greathouse

you call me out as fruit because I am

a lad with pink lady atop my head

to be tiny target   I eat nothing

but granny smith   you mark me

light in the loafers   to become light

I eat only cox's   medium sized

apples are eighty calories   russets

are fat free   you teach me homo

in tongue of reduction

I juice myself   turn myself to cider

flammable   you brand me faggot which

means kindling   I learn to burn   my body

disappears when you say poof

Development

age fourteen   I am the first boy to come
into high school with a camera phone

lunchtime   behind the biology block
the lads want me to shoot them

to capture flexing   licked lips
grabbed groins   their pornstar poses

as I pretend to be a man who directs
look at me   go on   be sexy   play dirty

I show them the snaps
say I'll delete them but pocket these boys

like a rosary   run them through my fingers
take the cold screen to bed

hold their pixels against my flesh
to find myself warming to them

Ash

in the air-raid shelter of RE class
you lounge behind a desk on the right side
of the blue room   me on the left   our eyes
find each other over the sea of heads
all looking straight forward at the teacher
you make a vagina with your right thumb
forefinger   flick your tongue through the halo
I imagine your fingers to be my
anus   your tongue inside my hole

Section Twenty Eight

after Andrew McMillan.

I'm sixteen when I find you on Grindr
teenager too   we know we want something

other boys don't   we talk with our fingers
how it might feel   to caress your fibre

optic hand   kiss your electric lips
we meet for sex on Skype   grasp our pix

elated flesh   speak with mouths   we help
one another   to come into our own

The Red Forest

from dusk me and you camp erect purple
polyester two-man Disney palace

by a raging fire my boy hands sweat
as I watch your man hands connect the poles

you swig a can of Bud I sip we toast
pink marshmallows I rush on pyjamas

behind rose bush see you shrug off shirt shorts
strip to boxers oak thighs torso knuckles

wrapped round hot mug slip in green sleeping bags
lie by each other like draft excluders

I blush to hear you whisper about *birds*
you want *to hammer* I stutter about

boys I want to *wrestle* so you unzip
our sleep sacks open them like flies mount me

trap me between those thighs I want to shake
off solid weight of you on my chest but

can't we play fight panting puppies try out
new moves on each other you lock my head

inside Lynx-wet armpit I bite your neck
until we come to feel drained in silence

we unlock one another climb down
from each other you crawl back inside your

sleep sack zip it up like a mouth I lie
in my body bag pretend to snore

School Mates

after Caroline Bird

he turned to potatoes   like his old man
she turned to a nightclub then cold turkey

he popped   turned to a deflated football
she turned to an unwritten novella

he turned to haddock on ice dreaming
of dancing in the Great Barrier Reef

she turned to stethoscope   thermometer
trying to stop Mother dying again

he had a girl by mistake   when
trying not to love daddies   otters   bears

she turned to the thought of her fly boyfriend
eating some tart in cherry-red lip balm

he turned to a soldier waiting for Dad
to die   then they turned into Sarah

Shame's Stone

after Richard Scott

ages five to twenty-six   when a boy
stares   smirks   smiles   kisses   my face
flushes as blood rushes   pushes my shame
to the surface   a stone   at the centre of my
cherry   tart flesh surrounds a pit with kernel inside
the drilling worm that turns green apple red
I'm five a day   cricket ball small
shame rises   bobs on my body of
water   it unfolds like
a note passed around class   is my shame like
that boy from school   who passed that note around
who I didn't like then and don't like now
is my shame like the first boy I
dated   who made me hard   who sucked me dry
who shoved me to the side of my life   who
made me put pen to paper   to write him
sonnets   does my shame feel like
nineties comics   *Judge Dredd   Dandy*
from my childhood   juxtaposed images
actions   snatches of dialogue   something
I hang on to   but mean to throw away
a comic book baddie   nobody
can destroy   The Joker   hell bent
on taking me hostage   taking over
the city of my mind   superhero
who can turn shame's poison into petrol
into medicine   into poetry   all
these shamed selves live in me like annual rings
in sweet chestnut   I can't remember
who first threw shame's stone in the sea of me
but I remember each ripple

Recentre

I Google Maps High Kelling to Weybourne
57 minutes   this smartphone knows
I'm male   5 9   10 3   so thinks it knows
how long it will take me to walk   assumes
I won't mince it   or skip   strut   limp   I won't
be chased   *2.6 miles via Church Close*
the easy route is to take the straight road
walk the blue line   Google guesses I won't
follow my nose up dirt tracks but   I do
cruise through Kelling woods   *traveller's joy*
sweet violets   fungi   to find my own
passage in the arse end of North Norfolk
Android shouts *recentre*   I lose signal
I get lost   I reach my destination

To Camp

a found poem

temporary shelter

complex of constructs for recreation

a summer holiday programme

the supporters of a party doctrine

to lodge in an uncomfortable place

to stay outside

a fenced field for grazing

livestock assembling together to rest

a site where people are kept

base for refugees   travellers   soldiers

Self-Graft

inosculation is
a natural phenomenon

in which the trunks   branches   roots of two trees
grow together

it's most common
with trees of the same kind

the branches first grow separately
in proximity to each other until

they touch
then bark

abrades away
as the trees blow in the wind

they self-graft   grow together   expand
ambling alone through High Kelling woodland

I clock tree-carved cave art   your names in hearts
GS   GG   1997

were you two boys   both penknife sharp
who met in this woodland just to explore

did you find shelter in each other
did your trunks inosculate

limbs bending around one another
I kiss your names   I hug your hearts

My Queer Mind Goes for a Walk

after Jason Allen-Paisant.

when I saunter through Sandringham woodland
bluebells   blackberries   Golden Wonder
cheese and onion crisp packets   my body
passes other walkers on the straight path
my epidermis feels their peepers burn
questions into my flesh   as if I am
prey   predator   is that a queer body
among brambles   ivy   a broken bike
why does he mince through our woodland   is it
to cruise for sex
the sly foxes are at it like rabbits
in the dog rose   cow parsley   fag packets
I am here to wander   to exercise
to smell wet sedge   to hear jays squawk   to spy
muntjacs   badgers   squirrels   weasels   hedgehogs
who see me   as just another animal

Roadkill

cruising Cromer back lanes at dusk   I come
across squashed deer   oily blood a mirror

guts mixed with sticks and stones   wearing its heart
fluid body   couldn't run free from man

Protect the Beautiful Landscape

protect the beautiful landscape
that is your queer body

don't let them walk all over you
you are private property

don't let them pick on your petals
don't let them plant punches to grow bruises

don't let them erect fences around you
to break you down   to box you in

don't let them buy or sell you
don't let them build their towers of torment

don't let them pollute you with toxic shame
don't let them send you to war with yourself

How To Care For Your Pansies

a found poem

pansies prefer full sun   love shade
pansies are cold   hardy   bloom any time

the temperature is above freezing
avoid windswept   exposed locations

pansies like rich moist organic manure
bed your pansy in a hole deep enough

to fit the root without bending   breaking
fill the hole gently   firm down   water

pansies require regular hydration
to guarantee   colourful display

Stinkhorn

forest *phallus impudicus* common
stinkhorn mushrooms thrust up through mulch

bulbous bases hollow spongey creamy
honeycomb stems their slimy black olive

conical caps drenched in sticky *gleba*
many men find their stench putrid but like

a fly I am pulled to their hum to land
on their helmets suck their spores to be

soaked in their seeds to ride them to new earth
insert themselves lay roots shoot

Wild Flowers

Hoary Plantain   Corky Fruited Dropwort
Purple Loosestrife   Night Flowering Catchfly
you plants in the wrong place   I pick you up

unwanted in nature's man-made spaces
farm fields   backyards   public parks
I want you   I take you in my basket

how are your shades of green deemed unsightly
Mantis   Crocodile   Jungle
Neon   Hooker's   I press you between hard covers

I don't label you weeds   I name you
Hedge Bedstraw   Oxeye Daisy   Corncockle
Bladder Campion   Forget Me Not   Vetch

I preserve you   you wild flowers who thrive
in nature where you survive all seasons
each bud punching through mud to unclench tiny fists

to bloom eternally   long after man
who said you don't belong   *Tansy Scented Mayweed*
Cocksfoot   Timothy Upright   Shepherd's Purse

Rucreation

after Danez Smith

in the beginning   RuPaul says   let them
be light   without explaining who they are

day two   Ru styles the sky from black velvet
day three   Ru styles the sea from cyan sequins

Ru forms the earth from powdered foundation
Ru forms blue roses   pink trees   glitter grass

day four   Ru casts the sun   the moon   from spotlights
Ru casts the stars   Bassey   Baldwin   Divine

day five   Ru shapes sea life from fishy looks
Ru shapes airborne life from feather boas

day six   Ru births land animals from snakeskin shoes   fox furs   Ru births all humans   by

dragging up some humans   Ru moulds gurls then
Ru moulds boys by untucking some gurls   but

Ru tells them all   you are equal homo sapiens
forged from star dust   now go forth   be fruitful

taste all fruits in the garden of the world
and love yourselves   because if you can't

love yourselves   how can you love somebody else
can I get a *gay men* up in here   then

everyone shouts *gay men* at Mama Ru
day seven   Ru rests   binge watches *Drag Race*

How Queer I Live On Norfolk Coast

after Arielle Greenberg

a sudden gust turns the reed bed
to whispering sea
the wind blows me
to wander lonely as a queer

to see all these thick trunks
I climb them   belly-slide along their muscular arms
to gaze down on village people
tourists cruising   daddies hammering pegs

erect tents to camp   out in the sticks
duckies   otters
foxes   flies   free-ranging cocks
bushes   cottages   pansies   dirt tracks   dykes

everything always opening
always coming out

Burrow

at Cley Nature Reserve   I sit alone
to spy humans bark for car park spaces
push in the lunch van's queue for bacon baps
as they twitter on about migration
whilst capturing warblers   I clock a mole
wriggle from its burrow   an underworld
it shares with worms   rabbits   spiders   do they
live in a cross-species community
underground scene   where no one rabbits on
about how you don't hear native birdsong
or do they too exist in tribes   working
hibernating   ploughing their own furrows
worming their way onto each other's land

We're Animals

we're cubs
we're otters
we're up each other like rats up drain pipes
we take the bull by the horn
we're the worm that turned
we're the pink sheep of the family
we're a wolf in our Mum's clothing
we're a bee in Gran's bonnet
we're elephants in the room
we're flies on the wall
we're sitting ducks
we're scapegoats

Killing It

perched on the bar   waiting for the latest
I see two lads   twenties   muscles   skin fades
tight tees   trackies   trainers   man uniform
they glug gut-filtered Guinness   wolf
pork scratchings   they bark about
how they're making a living by *killing*
it as British Gas salesmen   how they have
bagged girlfriends who are both dead
gorgeous   how they *own them   smash them   slay them*
yapping about lovers as if they aren't
alive   as if they're Porsches   piñatas   hogs
snorting about passion as if committing acts
of grievous bodily harm   homicide
about love lives in the language of death
my cheekbones turns up   a vision in denim
I tell him that *I am living for his new hair*

Self-Harm

my Dad taught me men shave by twelve   I am
branded sissy as I don't   the only

beard I have is called Sophie   I ache to
scrape off peach fluff   peel my Adam's Apple

each follicle has its own blood supply
muscle and nerve   why do men cut life off

their own bodies   eighty per cent of wo
men desire their men to be clean shaven

anticipation of sex makes hair grow
faster   the average man can take up

to one hundred strokes to shear his entire
face of his mane to reveal the piglet

pink beneath   what is masculinity
but a plastic disposable razor

blade pulled on the self

The Comedy of Masculinity

sat in the quiet pub   waiting for him
to get the drinks   at another table
when their girlfriends have gone to the toilet

I see him   drape his arm over his mate's
shoulder   and then stroke his friend's face
not sexual   not romantic
affectionate

and thinking they don't have an audience
so don't have to act natural   to play the parts of men
on the seventies sitcom set that is this pub
masculinities slip

Steam Room

what brings you here

through red-lit steam

a straight hunk's voice in blue shorts

I want to lose my belly fat   tone up

on sweating walls the shadow of his head nodding

avoid sugar   don't eat past six   like me

a meaty hand pats pecs at me

I can't see his whole body in this darkness

would we even see each other

outside this room of steam

would we ever talk in daylight

on a pub-garden picnic bench

Greater Anglia train

if we weren't stripped of our differences

Gym Boys

in gyms I watch lads come
to work machines in this factory

to manufacture men   now Jaguar
Nestlé   coal mines   have shut

spot them   newbie   gym bunny   jock   players
stock characters   *alright fellas*   a script

what you working on now   as if they're thesps
leg day   could be a fringe play   Above The Stag

they get in position   grab props   dumbbells
perform their set in reps   play to the gods

in the mirror   I spy *natural blokes*
acting macho   self-harm   rip tissue

to break themselves
down while other boys watch

to tell one another how fit they are
now they can't tell women

how hot they are   now birds
never tell blokes   to get the perfect male body

to get bigger
harder

I row
breathe

the pants
of hunk

who pulls
who pushes

himself
beside me

I take in
his puff

which has pumped
all round

his blood
to cock

to heart
I suck him in

swallow him down
a sort

of blow
or snog

or mouth
to mouth

then they finish
wipe dry their heads on raised tees before

staring at their own
reflections in full-length mirrors

wash in the showers together like lovers
shamed schoolboys scrubbing away the game

Straitjacket

from birth you're locked in a blue straitjacket
forged from canvas   duck cloth   your sleeves sewn shut

to restrict fingers from playing with boys
lipstick   ovens   to stop your wrists limping

arms crossed against the chest   a coffined corpse
the ends of cuffs strapped to the back of the

chameleon camisole   becomes grey
Paul Smith blazer   bloody rugby shirt   gym vest

Masculinity Is A Drag

category is construction realness
on the pavement's catwalk   tradesmen werk it

heeled boots   big belts   neon vests   helmets
made up in dusty powder   smeared in oil

doing their routine   glossing   gluing   skirting
filling   drilling   pumping   grinding   smashing

all lip-syncing to the same old pop song
gagging on shade thrown at one another

builder's T is everywhere
their feelings tucked

Shaggy

there are several types of bear   Spectacled
Giant Panda   Polar   Sloth   adult males

have large bodies   stocky legs   small rounded
ears   shaggy hair   big paws   for bears   staring

is an aggressive act   bears snort   moan   blow
tongue lick   jaw click   lip pop   bears claw

bears rub themselves up against trees to leave
their scent   to mark territory   bears like

to dominate   bears love fresh meat   bears feast
on anything   bears are hunted   their flesh

their fur   in subcultures   bears are worshipped
bears are seen as father figures   bears are

sometimes made to bop for entertainment
bears   cubs   don't just live in forests   Google

defines bear as mammal   toy   to carry
a weight   to be rugged   shaggy man's man

This Gay Club Is My Church

I come here religiously   I come for
confession   I come for confirmation
I come for love   I come for communion
I come to praise Him   Him   Her   Them   Me   Us
I come to worship our Lady Gaga
I come to sing hymns to the Madonna
I come to dance   I come to bask in light
I come to cast away the devil shame
I come to kneel   I come to kiss his ring
I come to take his flesh inside my mouth
I come to feel him enter me   I come
to feel him inside me   I come to feel
him move in mysterious ways
for what I'm about to receive

Queen

alone during COVID 19 lockdown
I trudge away the days through Runton woods

dreaming the ten-watt sun to be pink strobe
thick fog to be dry ice   hot breath   raindrops

to be glitter   wet ground to be sticky
with sweat   spilt shots   longing to find a mate

then I hear him   a bee   fizzing with want
male bees are drones who live to mate with queens

I see him   in yellow-black fur   waspish
I watch him buzz round heather   rosemary

bees communicate by waggle dancing
to show other bees where the nectar is

part of a colony   but not right now
happy   drinking in the natural world

smell spilt Jack Daniels   Tennessee honey
the fog becomes dry ice   the sun a strobe

Mince

mincer   does his screaming spinning-blade barb
cut   dice   shred me into tiny pieces

to mince   *to walk with short quick steps*
can I take long strides in his world   do I

pass smart so meatheads won't claw me   my blood
battles itself   takes flight to heart   *when meat*

is minced   bruised tissue releases juices
to flavour sauce   is my mince my nature

just as lambs spring   do sissies skip their way
to the grinder   do I mince to align

my trot with my unsavoury appetites
for a true mince   the effect   to fashion

closely bonded mixture   a soft texture
is mincing learnt bearing   cocks have taught this

chick how to strut   do I mince to peacock
erect my tail   demonstrate to possible mates

or is mincing a march   a flamboyance
of flamingos march in tight groups   heads high

when they flock together   they're called a stand
is my mince camo   eggshell   nest   battle

cry   begging call   bird song   a pheromone
secreted by skin glands to mark my state

Queer Time

in G A Y   he waits   a wing-clipped parakeet
every Saturday night   drunk on the view

gazing at twinks as if he's one of them
glaring at bears   as if he's one of them

he's been eighteen for ten years now   never
dropped the balls   grown out of hair on the chests

a forever-hatching chrysalis
a wolf in Generation Z's skinnies

don't we all live in three tenses at once?
memories present in our wants

his headmaster still won't let him love men
Thatcher still forbids a pretend family

his body clock will never strike baby
so how   why   when   will his watch stop

Grind

a found poem from Grindr profiles

hey hi I'm just looking not looking
for anything in particular I don't know
what I'm looking for I want a friend a
gaping hole daddy cum hungry mouth
husband a top bottom couple seeking
third party fuckboi no strings I just want
fun don't be old young I want someone
to get high with drunk with no alkies be a boozer
someone for the theatre for dinner no chubs
be chiselled muscly six pack gymboi someone
for netflix and chill don't be lazy ambitious
outdoorsy someone to go out with don't be
sceney someone to stay in with but not
a faggot sissy no camps be out be straight
acting when you fuck me suck me don't be
mental be sane be smart no students career driven
be a driver have a good sense of humour don't
be tory artsy fascist woke closet uber-liberal
be on the property ladder don't live
with parents be willing to travel I can
accommodate no Blacks no Asians it's not
racist it's just a type I want bears otters
no pets I'm allergic be a dog lover
no pic no chat have a face if I don't
reply I don't fancy you you're not
my type you're ugly it's nothing
personal

Sand/Sea

a spot that receives less than ten inches
of rain per year is pronounced a dust bowl

in bed   watch abs undress   reveal hourglass
figure   I turn him over   I bury

my head in him   sand sticks like
nothing else   the beach aches for someone's footprints

shore is a finite resource   animals
can't make a home in sand   he slips through my

fingers   I wave goodbye   sand is broken
down rocks battered over the years by waves

/

you call to me and I come crawling back
you wave and I undress
you lick then lap then pull me in
smash me
you edge   closer   closer   peak heap curl then
explode
and hurl your load all over the shore then
you collapse onto the sea bed
whisper sweet somethings as you slide out
slither away
leaving me stung
shivering
feeling insignificant
longing for god knows what

Mutual

stripped bare on the queen sized   your left thigh
draped all over mine   I become your right hand

you'd self-abuse with when you were
under covers at night petrified you'd never come

out   you turn to my right which wrote
sci-fi in ruled grey schoolbooks that ached

as I felt alien   we stroke our slugs
awake to eels   electric blood

squeeze our girth like cucumbers
buff each other up   gold lamps

cocktail shake one another until
ready to pour   inside my hand

I feel your sperm surge up   we explode
on each others wrists   chef's kiss

Nuts and Bolts

after Thom Gunn

I stir from sleep   wake in the bed we built
in which we fart and fuck and watch football

to find myself in your vice-like cuddle
your arm a taut seatbelt across my chest

our fingers interlinked dovetailed timber
my shoulder superglued to your armpit

your solid stomach soldered to my spine
your bolt-like cock screwed to my nut-tight butt

our heavy legs tangled like long link chain
and in your grip I am solid   strong   safe

I slide back in to sleep and think how wrong
are those blokes who say men's bodies don't fit

Birdcage

penguins are unable to fly   queer birds
I think as my other half and I look

from sign to cage   *Ronnie   Reggie*   couple
of male migrant Humboldts we humans have

branded gay when they adopted an egg
smirking teen boy films them   spots me and Jake

holding hands   an act penguins can't perform
boy throws us *fags*   as if it's a herring

he wants us to bite   I snap back *virgin*
Humboldts have spines on their tongues to hold prey

teen boy toddles to grizzly Mum and Dad
who push their young in prams   they point and stare

captivated by the captive love birds
we wobble in our invisible cage

Spill

I am thirteen when hit for being found
in possession of gay mag *Attitude*
the average adult penis is thirteen
centimetres when erect   at twenty
I ask my boyfriend to hit me as we
have sex   when the cause of death is hanging
the male often gets an erection called
death erection   angel lust   my boyfriend
won't cry when hit on a night out clubbing
as *men don't cry*   there are three columns of
tissue that run inside the penis   my
boyfriend won't say sorry when he strikes me
with his elbow and spills his colleague's drinks
the penis is spineless   no baculum
only blood pressure to stay erect   my
boyfriend jokes   *I love my car more than you*
the average speed of ejaculation
is twenty-eight miles per hour
blood is loaded in two cylinder shaped
chambers causing the penis to stiffen
my boyfriend is addicted to the gym
he says   *cos I'm a man and men should be*
muscly   though the penis contains none

Heart Attack

the heart weighs a pound   you spend ninety nine
pence on my Lidl Valentine's Day card

unlike other cells   heart cells don't divide
my heart is the same size as two hands clasped

you won't hold my hand in public in case
we get beaten   my heart beats one hundred

and fifteen thousand times each day   you said
I love you once   Monday is the day when

most heart attacks happen   on Christmas Day
you leave me for a man in New Jersey

if you were to stretch out my blood vessels
they extend over sixty thousand miles

the smallest mammal   the American
Pygmy Shrew   has the fastest beating heart

Gaysthetics

I prefer the glossy magazine
to the moist men between the covers   I
can always finish *Attitude*   I
was not taught I *have an inalienable right*
to be gay   I prefer the sex
in Bacon paintings   where bodies dissolve
to sand   red mist   fancy gold heels
queen-blue dresses   candy floss pink feathers
on the drag queen to the boy tucked beneath
no skirt ever punched me   called me *sissy*
no *authority promoted homo*
sexuality   I prefer Gucci
floral wallpaper hanging in his
bedroom   to hanging in his bedroom
long bus rides to bedsits with an atmos
phere of frustration   stilted torturous con
versation until you get to the point
do I have to lift his shirt   bite pillows
I prefer the hankies in back pockets
to back passages   I'd plump for the d
iamond ring to the thought of
slipping my finger in   *pretended family*
relationships   I'd rather read Orton's
juicy journals than to catch cold cruising
the men he slept with   every *faggot* comes
from a man   how do I want who I am
scared of wanting   I prefer to watch
Chalamet   Hammer   than to hammer them
fat   feet   blood   shit   shame   *the virus*
can be passed during sexual
intercourse with an infected person
sex kills   I've buried my lust in poems

Tickled Pink

Cotton Candy Pink
Is desire strawberry ice cream / marshmallows / cotton candy
/ macaroons with raspberries?

Precious Pink
Brazilian pink topaz / Tanzanian pink sapphire / Moroccan
calcite?

Capitalist Pink
A 1963 Pink Cadillac / the modernist pink skyscraper
Georgia-Pacific Tower in Atlanta?

Professional Pink
A pink collar worker / the pink pound / a pink slip?

Baby Pink
Is desire Baby Spice's pink dress? Age five, I see it and want it /
but what do I want / Baby Spice / what lies beneath her baby
pink dress / to be Baby Spice / to wear that pink dress this
baby already knows they're forbidden to wear?

Uniform Pink
In 19th century England, pink ribbons and clothes were
worn by boys considered to be small men / as men wore
red uniforms / boys wore pink ones / is desire 19th Century /
small men / red uniforms?

War Pink
Blue and pink were first used as gender signifiers just before
World War One / pink established as a feminine colour by
the 1940s / is desire gender / a world war / a world / stuck in
the 1940s?

Eisenhower Pink

In 1953, at Eisenhower's presidential inauguration, his wife Mamie wore a pink dress / this was a key turning point in the association of pink with girls / is desire a president / an inauguration / a wife / a pink dress / a thought / a key / a turning point?

Confirmation Pink

In art, pink is the colour associated with the body of Christ / age twelve, do I worship school mate Jake / under my bed I make a secret shrine / his stolen gym shorts, rugby shirt, gum shield / is desire religious / confession / communion / confirmation?

Frogfish Pink

The pink ocelated frogfish / camouflaged to look like a rock covered in algae / ages 12-17, this pink frogfish camouflaged himself in red rugby shirts to look like a rock / but other rocks saw him / they made him black and blue / is desire camouflage that fails / a rock?

Cochineal Pink

Carmine pink food colouring / made from crushed insects called cochineals / is desire food / colouring / crushing / an insect?

Punched Pink

The verb 'to pink' dates from the 14th century / meaning 'to decorate with a perforated or punched pattern' / is desire a verb / does it date / is it decoration / a pierced tongue or colander / does it punch / does it follow a pattern?

Iguana Pink

The pink iguana of the Galapagos Islands / first identified in 1986 / first recognised as a distinct species in 2009 / did I first identify my desire in 1997 / age 4 I colour my nails with pink felt-tip pen / or when in 2008 age 15 I pull off Ashley under the desk at the back of the Chemistry lab / or when in 2010 age 17 I tell my parents / I'm... a distinct species...?

Sheep Pink

Boy George famously said he 'was the pink sheep of the family'.

Legal Pink

In England and Wales, a brief delivered to a barrister by a solicitor is tied with pink ribbon / pink was traditionally the colour associated with the defence / is desire brief / briefs / delivered / a barrister / tied with ribbon / defence / defensive / a legal issue / my desire is illegal in 70 countries / punishable by death in 12 / unlike my baby-pink suitcase / my right to publicly express my desire / can't travel round the world with me.

Triangle Pink

Inmates of Nazi concentration camps accused of being homosexual were forced to wear a pink triangle / now a reclaimed symbol of the gay rights movement / is desire a concentration camp / a triangle / a symbol / a right / a movement?

In The Pink

In Japan, pink is most commonly associated with spring time / blooming cherry blossoms / is desire spring / cherry blossom / Chris White popped my cherry in April 2013 / was I in the pink / tickled pink?

Butt Cheek Pink

Is desire the deep pink of Chris' butt cheeks / the French
pink of Sean's lips / the steel pink of Jake's helmet / the
piggy pink of Jason's face when he called me queer / the
hot pink of my cheeks' blush?

Red Pink

Pink is a pale tint of red / does my vanilla stop me being
Fire Engine / does shame stop me being Chocolate Cosmos
/ am I scared to be Blood?

Elephant Pink

Jack London wrote that to hallucinate from alcohol is to
'see pink elephants' / is desire hallucination / rosé / to see
pink elephants?

Outsiders

after Kei Miller

behind bushes of ripe leaves
drooping like limp wrists
I enter the warrens of dark
dripping meandering corridors
to a place between places   a nowhere
an everywhere   an other world inside
this world   a wild life within the wildlife
where we fallen fruit trees   all uprooted
bearing our rings   create a club within
the scrub   I kneel in front of him   his fly
cracks open like a chrysalis
then the slow unrolling
I plant my mouth
inhale   exhale   my breath
passes through his body of water
until we become a shower
of dandelion seeds   we wish
to reclaim our nature
to be out in the open
to be outsiders
to be easy outside in our bodies

Gardening

in Sheringham   I have a small cottage
garden that spills onto the shingle beach

the only wall that borders it is horizon
I plant pansies   tie-dyed roses

green carnations   violets
rainbow wallflowers

I want Creeping Charlie to overrun
flora   take up space   coalesce   create

new forms   in my Eden   I'm God   Mother
Nature   no one forbidden entry   fruit

Notes and Acknowledgements

'Closet' and 'Joe' were first published in *Impossible Archetype*. Joe is dedicated to JM: I'm sorry.

'Intestines' was Commended in the York Poetry Prize 2021 judged by Dr Kim Moore.

'The Weight' was first published in Cephalo Press and is written after torrin a. greathouse.

'Seed' was first published as 'Urinals' in *The Cardiff Review*.

'Development' was first published as 'Camera Phone' in The *Butcher's Dog* and reprinted in *Impossible Archetype*.

'Ash' is dedicated to Ashley Squires. Thank you for twenty five years of friendship.

'Section 28' is written after Andrew McMillan.

'School Mates' is written after Caroline Bird.

'Self-Graft' was first published as 'Inosculation' in *Finished Creatures* and Lines 1-13 are adapted from Wikipedia's article on inosculation. This one is dedicated to Finn Anderson who sent me a photo of insoculating trees which inspired this poem.

'Shame's Stone' was first published in *Fourteen Poems* and is written after Richard Scott.

'To Camp' is a found poem using text sourced from a Google search of the phrase 'to camp'.

'To Camp', 'How To Care For Your Pansies', 'Stinkhorn', 'Burrow' and 'Roadkill' were all first published in UEA's *Speculative Nature Writing Anthology*.

'My Queer Mind Goes For A Walk' was first published in *You Are Here: The Queer Ecologies Journal of Creative Geography* and is written after Jason Allen-Paisant.

'Protect The Beautiful Landscape' was first published in *Maw Poetry Magazine* and reprinted in *force/field* anthology.

'How To Care For Your Pansies' is a found poem using text sourced on BBC Gardening's page on pansies.

'Wild Flowers' was first published in *Finished Creatures* and reprinted in *You Are Here: The Queer Ecologies Journal of Creative Geography*.

'Rucreation' is written after Danez Smith and was first published in *Poetry Wales*.

'How Queer I Live On Norfolk Coast' was first published in *You Are Here: The Queer Ecologies Journal of Creative Geography* and is written after Arielle Greenberg.

'We're Animals' was first published in *Lunate*.

'Self-Harm' was first published as 'Shave' in *The Alchemy Spoon*.

'The Comedy of Masculinity' was first published as 'Humans' in *Popshot Quarterly*.

'Gym Boys' is dedicated to my gym boy Cameron McFarlene.

'Shaggy' was first published as 'Bears' in Cephalo Press.

'This Gay Club Is My Church' was first published in *Queerlings* and won Poetry Archive's World View Competition 2021.

'Queen' was first published in *Shooter Literary Journal*.

'Mince' in part borrows text found in a Google search of 'mince' and text from BBC Good Food's mince page. It was first published in *Under The Radar*.

'Queer Time' was first published in *The North*.

'Mutual' and 'Nuts and Bolts' are dedicated to Aaron Scott-Carter.

'Nuts and Bolts' was first published in *Nightsweats: Art and Poetry After Gunn's Nightsweats* published by Guillaume Vandame.

'Spill' was first published as 'Penis' in *Brag Magazine.*

'Heart Attack' was first published as 'Heart' in Tealight Press.

'Gaysthetics' was Commended in The Waltham Forest Poetry Competition 2021 judged by Joelle Taylor.

'Tickled Pink' borrows and adapts facts from Wikipedia's page on the colour pink.

'Outsiders' is written after Kei Miller.

'Gardening' was first published in *Anthropocene* and reprinted in *You Are Here: The Queer Ecologies Journal of Creative Geography.* It is dedicated to the memory of Derek Jarman.

Earlier drafts of 'Intestines', 'The Weight', 'Shame's Stone', 'We're Animals', 'My Queer Mind Goes For A Walk', 'Shaggy', 'Self-Graft', 'Queen', 'Wild Flowers', 'How Queer I Live On Norfolk Coast' and 'Gardening' were first published in my pamphlet *Green Apple Red*, Broken Sleep Books, 2022.

Thanks

Thanks to these publications and their editors for seeing something in my poems and giving them homes.

Thanks to Arts Council England for a Developing Your Creative Practice Grant which gave me the space, time and funds to write and research this collection with mentoring from Richard Scott.

Thanks to Richard Scott for his galvanising, patient, insightful, process-changing mentoring and support over the last three years.

Thanks to Anthony Anaxagorou, Rachel Long and Remi Graves and all who participated on their respective courses Advanced Poetry Workshop, Writing Desire and Writing Queer Sex ran with Poetry School, where several of these poems were written and workshopped.

Thanks to Jane Commane at Nine Arches Press for publishing this book and for her thorough thoughtful faithful editing of these poems.

Thanks to fellow queer eco-poet Caleb Parkin whose suggested reading, encouragement and cyber friendship inspired the writing of this collection.

Thanks to Caleb, Jo Bell, Paul Stephenson, Rick Dove, and Richard Scott for writing generous endorsements.

Thanks to my mum Marie and my best mates Aaron, Mark, Dawn, David, Marcus, Jeni, Pasco and Lucy for their support, encouragement and friendship during the writing of this collection.

This collection is dedicated to the memory of my father Shaun McDermott who aged sixty died of COVID 19 during the writing of this book. Thank you for teaching me how to read and write. All this is your fault.